... loves to read God's Word.

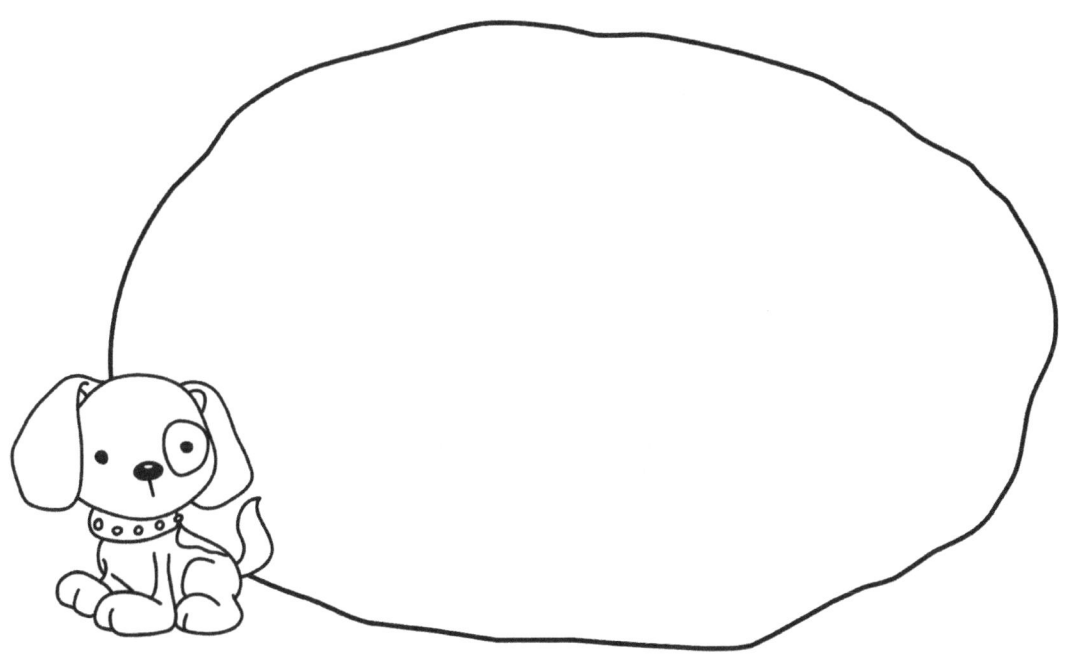

Draw a picture of yourself.

iCharacter

Published by iCharacter Ltd.
www.icharacter.org
By Agnes and Salem de Bezenac
Illustrated by Agnes de Bezenac
Copyright. All rights reserved.
All Bible verses adapted from the KJV.

Copyright © 2015 iCharacter Limited. All rights reserved. No part of this book may be reproduced in any form or by any electronic or mechanical means, including information storage and retrieval systems, without written permission from the publisher or author, except in the case of a reviewer, who may quote brief passages embodied in critical articles or in a review.

God Makes the World

When God created the world, He took great care and effort to make it just right for you and me to enjoy. When God finished, He was very pleased with His good work.

(Read Genesis 1)

A Hidden Message

Color all of the boxes that have one dot to find the hidden message.

A Sad Mistake

God told Adam and Eve that they could eat fruit from any tree in the Garden except for one. But they didn't control themselves and ate it anyway. This made God sad.

(Read Genesis 3:6)

Trace and Match

Trace over the words, color the pictures and then draw a line to make pairs.

Noah Follows God

When God told Noah to build a big boat for his family and all the animals, Noah paid close attention, followed God's instructions and did exactly what God told him to do.

(Read Genesis 6:13-22)

Find the Pairs

Help Mr. Noah find two of each animal that are exactly alike.

The Very Tall Tower

Some people were so proud and thought they could build a great big tower to reach up to God. But no one can be as good as God. God mixed up their languages and they had to stop working.

(Read Genesis 11:1-9)

Different Languages

Match the country with its language by coloring the bricks the same color.

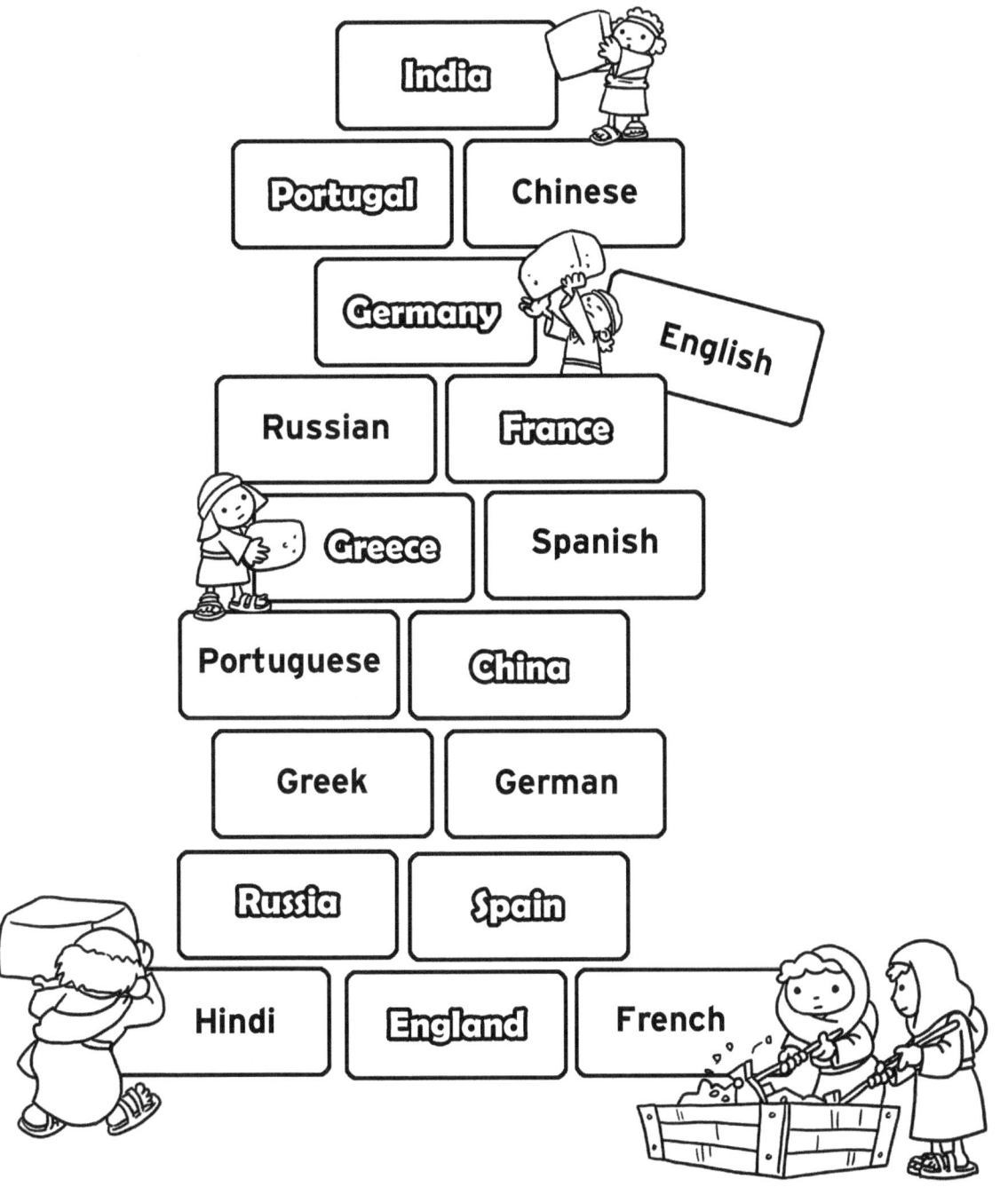

Abraham Depends on God

Abraham didn't know where to go. He prayed and depended on God's help and guidance. Abraham listened and followed Him. God always knows what's best for us, doesn't He?

(Read Genesis 12:1-9)

Help Find the Way

Help Abraham find his way through the maze to find God's will and where to set up his tent and new home.

Waiting for a Baby

Abraham and Sarah wanted a baby. They waited patiently for many years. Even though it took a long time and they got old, God kept His promise and blessed them with a cute baby boy.

(Read Genesis 15-18; 21:1-7)

How Old?

Find out how old Abraham was when he learned that Sarah was going to have baby Isaac by starting from the left and writing every second letter in the blanks.
How old are you? Draw the right number of candles in the box.

_ _ _ _ _ _ _ _ _ _

A Wife for Isaac

Abraham's servant chose Rebekah to be Isaac's wife because she took the initiative and gave all the camels water to drink. She saw a need and did something about it.

(Read Genesis 24)

Who Am I?

Read the descriptions below and put a ✓ on the ones you think apply to Rebekah. Put an X if you feel they don't apply. Then color the girl that you think became Isaac's wife.

- didn't give water to the servant
- gave water to one camel
- selfish
- angry voice
- frowning
- carried a suitcase

- gave water to the servant
- gave water to all the camels
- helpful
- soft voice
- smiling
- carried a water pot

Jacob Cheats

Jacob cheated and tricked his father into giving him the blessing, instead of to his brother Esau. Later, Jacob was sorry and sad because he knew that what he had done was wrong.

(Read Genesis 25, 27)

What Did Jacob Learn?

To find out, go through the path and collect the letters as you go.

_ _ _ _ _ _ _ _ _ _ _ _ _ _ _ _

Jacob Has a Dream

God gave Jacob a dream to encourage him and show him that He still loved him. God forgave him even after he made the mistake of cheating his brother.

(Read Genesis 28:10-22)

Up the Stairs

Join the number dots, then finish the pictures of the angel, and Jacob sleeping.

Joseph's Colorful Coat

"It's not fair!" Joseph's brothers shouted. "Why does Joseph get a new coat and we don't?" They were jealous and wanted what Joseph had. But, later, they were sorry and learned to be content.

(Read Genesis 37, 39-46)

Fashion Designer

Make patterns on Joseph's new coat, then color it.

Miriam Does Her Part

Miriam watched over her little brother, Moses, while he was hiding in the Nile river. She looked out for him to make sure that he was safe. Miriam learned to be responsible.

(Read Exodus 2:1-10)

Spot the Differences

Circle the differences from the picture on the left. There are 15.

25

Crossing the Red Sea

Moses stretched out his hands and prayed. God made a path through the sea and all the people walked through on dry ground. "Thank You, God, for this miracle!" the people shouted.

(Read Exodus 13-15)

Be the Artist

Finish drawing the picture of Moses and God's people crossing the Red Sea.
Or, if you prefer, glue some blue paper strips on either side of them for the sea.

God's Commandments

God gave Moses "Ten Commandments" to pass on to the people. God wanted them to follow and obey these rules because He knew that they were good for them and would make them happy.

(Read Exodus 20)

Fill in the Blanks

Fill in the blanks to help you remember the Ten Commandments.
Cross out the words from the list as you go.

1. Love God _____ than anything else
2. Don't make anything more important than _____
3. Use God's _____ with love and respect
4. Take a day to _____
5. Love and _____ your parents
6. Don't _____ anyone
7. Be faithful to your _____ or wife
8. Don't take _____ that aren't yours
9. Always tell the _____
10. Be _____ with what you have

truth
hurt
name
things
content
more
respect
husband
rest
God

29

The Battle of Jericho

Joshua was eager and ready to follow God's instructions in order to take over Jericho.
Even though it seemed a little silly and crazy at first, Joshua was willing to obey.

(Read Joshua 5-6)

Into Jericho at Last!

Help Joshua get into the city of Jericho.

Deborah Goes into Battle

God's people needed help. Even though going into battle wasn't something that women usually did, Deborah was glad to be of service. God helped her and His people to win the battle.

(Read Judges 4-5)

True or False

Read the text boxes, then draw a line to the TRUE box or the FALSE box.

- Deborah was a judge.
- Deborah took the best for herself.
- Deborah decided not to go.
- Deborah listened to God's instructions.
- God chose Deborah to help lead the army.
- Women always went into battle.
- Deborah helped people find solutions.
- Deborah gladly served God's people.
- With God's help the victory was won.
- Deborah sang a song of praise.

True

False

God Helps Gideon

God told Gideon to do some things that were different and a bit odd, but Gideon trusted Him. He showed himself flexible as he changed his own plans to follow God's plans.

(Read Judges 6-7)

Story Words

Color in all the words that have something to do with the story of Gideon.

PENCIL

Gideon trust

DOG RAMSHORN

TENT GAME

TORCH night

jars VICTORY

SNACK SCHOOL

Samson the Strong

Samson was a judge who helped God's people. He learned the importance of making wise decisions and not only doing what he felt like doing.

(Read Judges 13, 16)

From Where?

From where did Samson get his true strength?

Ruth Honors Naomi

Ruth didn't want Naomi to be on her own. Ruth showed faithfulness as she stayed to help and take care of her, just as family should. God blessed Ruth in many ways.

(Read the Book of Ruth)

Corns of Wheat

Count the heads of wheat. How many are there?

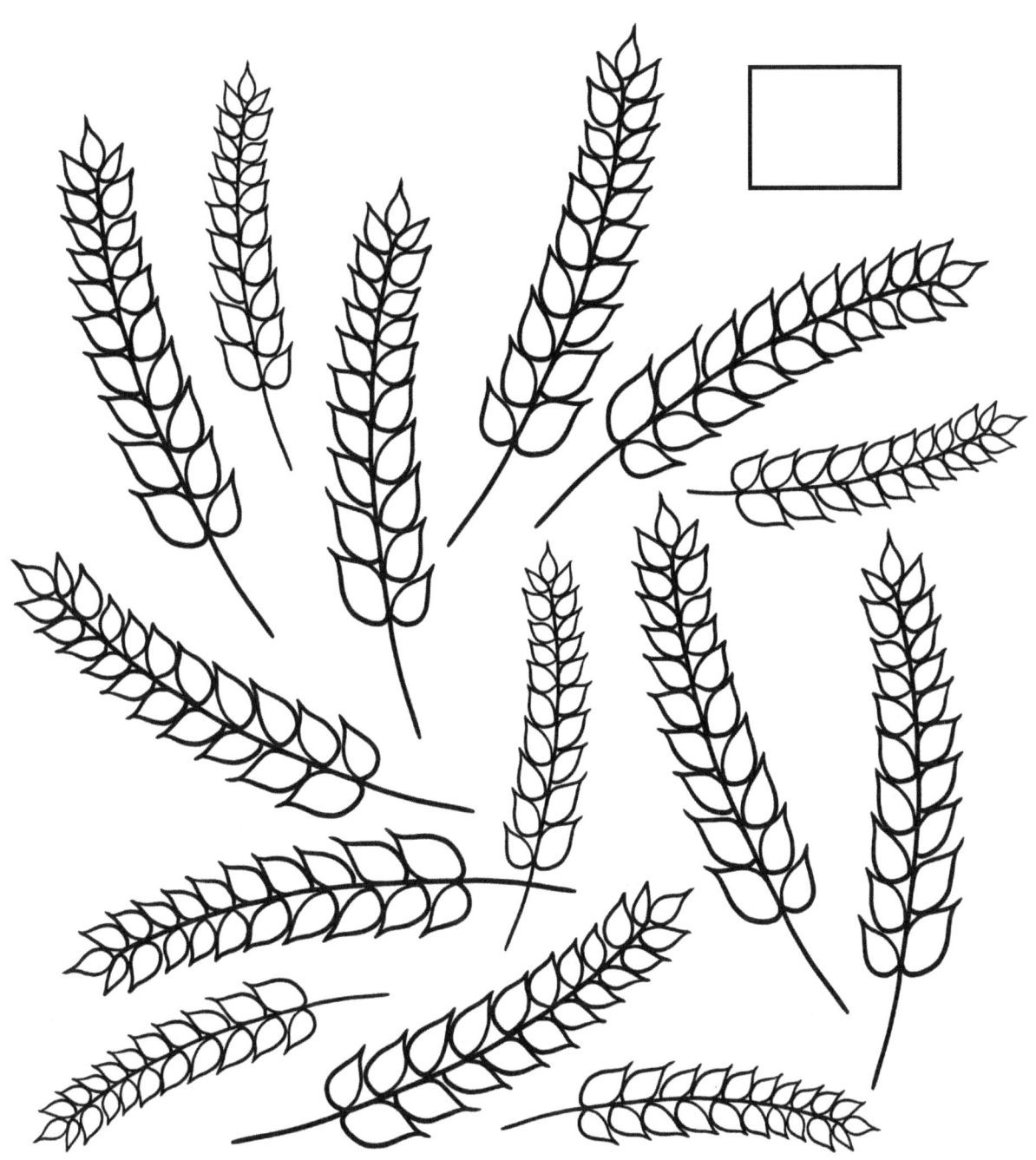

Hannah Thanks God

God blessed Hannah with a son and this made her so happy! She thanked and praised God over and over again. "I praise You, God! You are great! You are awesome!" she said.

(Read 1 Samuel 1-2:11)

Find the Match

Look closely and circle the picture that is exactly like the example in the circle.

41

Samuel Listens

Samuel learned how to pray and listen to God when he was just a boy.
He stayed very still and quiet so that he could hear God's important messages.

(Read 1 Samuel 3:1-19)

What Did Samuel Do?

Color the letters with a dot inside to see what Samuel did.

Samuel... PRAYED

A Shepherd Boy

Young David cared for his father's sheep. He took them on long walks so they could find fresh water and green grass. He also kept them safe from danger and wild animals.

(Read 1 Samuel 16)

Be the Artist

Learn how to draw one of David's little lambs by following each step.

Draw your cute lamb in here:

Fighting a Big Man

Everyone was afraid of the big giant Goliath. But David said, "I will fight the giant with God's help. With God, I am not afraid. With God, I have courage!"

(Read 1 Samuel 17)

Questions and Answers

Color the correct picture to match each question.

How old was David in this story?

What did Goliath look like?

What did David use to fight Goliath?

David's Songs to God

King David wrote many songs to show his love and thanks to God. "The Lord is my shepherd and gives me everything that I need. He leads me on the right path ..." David sang.

(Read Psalm 23)

Follow the Path

Discover one of David's songs by following the path and reading the words in order.

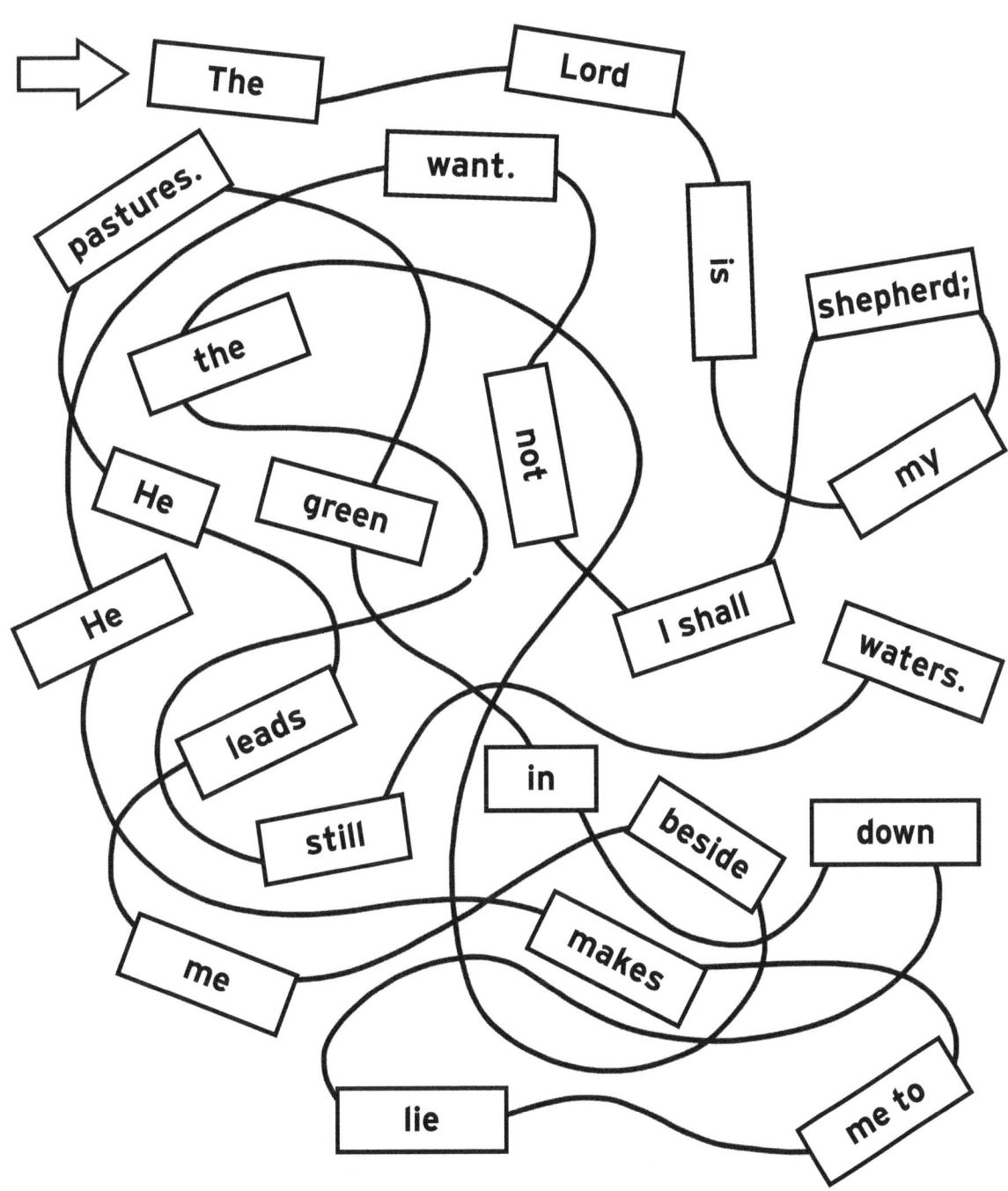

49

King Solomon Is Wise

When Solomon became king, he knew that he needed God's help to rule well. So, he prayed and asked for extra wisdom, even more than for riches and power.

(Read 1 Kings 3:3-15)

What Is Wisdom?

Draw a line from the gold coins of wise things to do to the chest. Then color them in.

- I take time with God.
- I do something nice for my neighbor.
- I look out for myself first.
- I'm honest and tell the truth.
- I give and share with others.
- I get angry when I don't get my way.
- I think more about others.
- I fight to win, so that others don't.
- I cheerfully obey my parents.

Having wisdom is like having great riches.

Building a Temple

King Solomon built a beautiful temple so that the people could worship God there. When the temple work was complete, they celebrated with a praise party.

(Read 1 Kings 5-7)

Praises to God

Welcome to Solomon's temple! If you were there, what would you thank God for? Write whatever comes to mind in the speech bubbles below.

God Feeds Elijah

Elijah hid from bad Queen Jezebel who wanted to hurt him. God took care of Elijah and sent birds to bring him food each day. Elijah waited patiently for many days until it was safe to leave again.

(Read 1 Kings 17:1-7)

God Provides

What did God provide for Elijah while he hid?

bread   **water**   **meat**

A Widow in Need

There was a famine and Elijah was hungry. He went to a poor widow who showed unselfishness and gave him her last little bread. God did a miracle and blessed her with much more.

(Read 1 Kings 17:7-16)

What Happened?

There is a hidden word in each row. Circle the words and you'll find the happy ending to the story.

t	t	t	t	h	e	t	t	t	t
w	w	w	w	w	i	d	o	w	s
r	f	l	o	u	r	r	r	r	r
n	n	n	n	n	n	a	n	d	n
i	i	i	i	i	o	i	l	i	i
d	d	i	d	d	d	d	d	d	d
o	o	o	o	n	o	t	o	o	o
u	u	u	u	u	u	u	r	u	n
o	u	t	t	t	t	t	t	t	t

Naaman Gets Help

Naaman was sick with leprosy. Elisha told him to go and wash in the river seven times. Naaman really wanted to get better, and so he washed again and again, seven times. He obeyed God and he was healed.

(Read 2 Kings 5:1-15)

Find the Shapes

These shapes are taken from the picture on the left.
Tick them off as you find them in the picture.

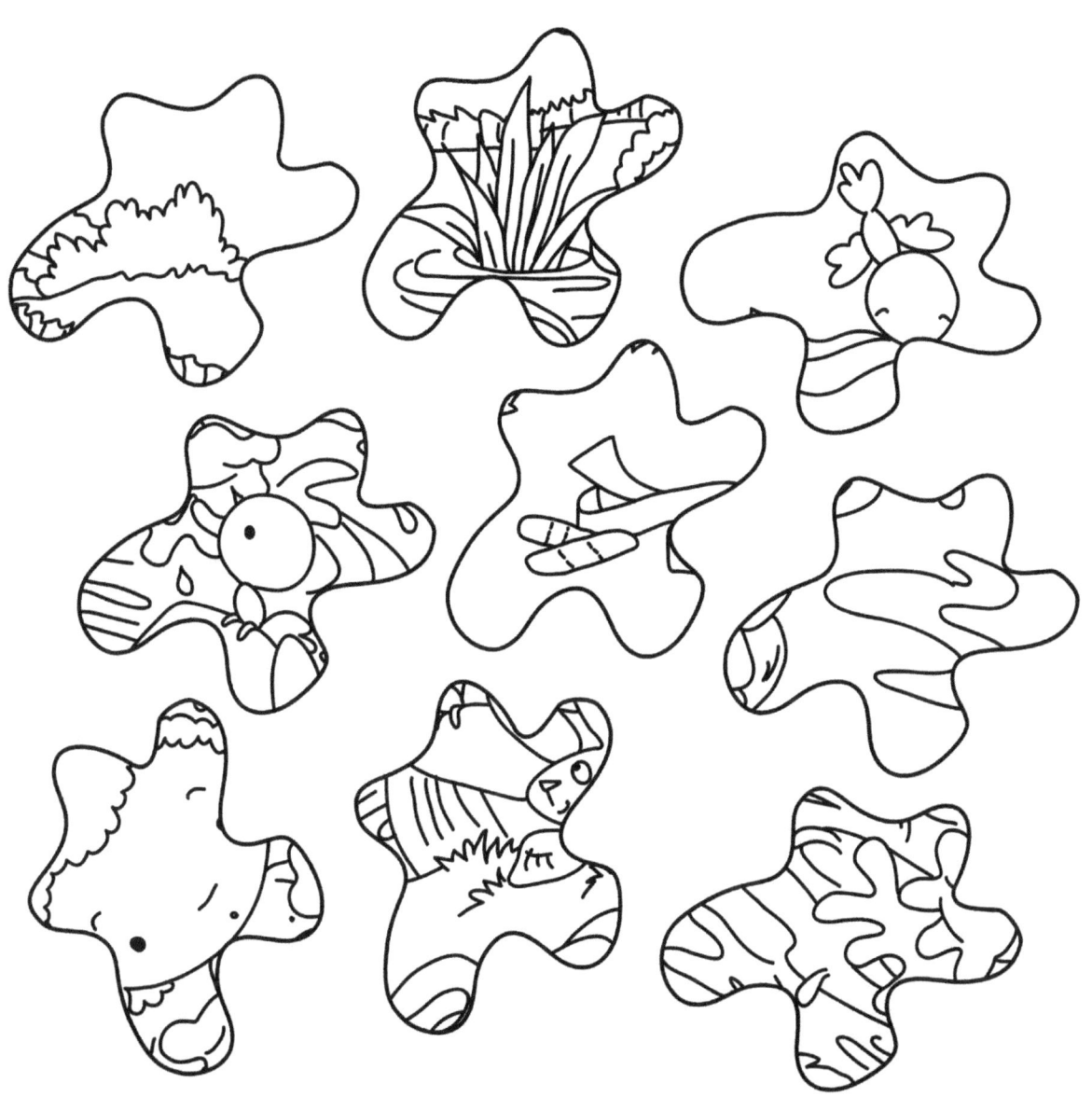

Little King Joash

Little boy Joash became king at only seven years old. It was a big job to be the king, so he needed lots of help and advice. He learned to work well with others and listen to their suggestions.

(Read 2 Kings 11-12)

Dot-to-Dot

Complete the two dot-to-dot pictures, then color your favorite one.

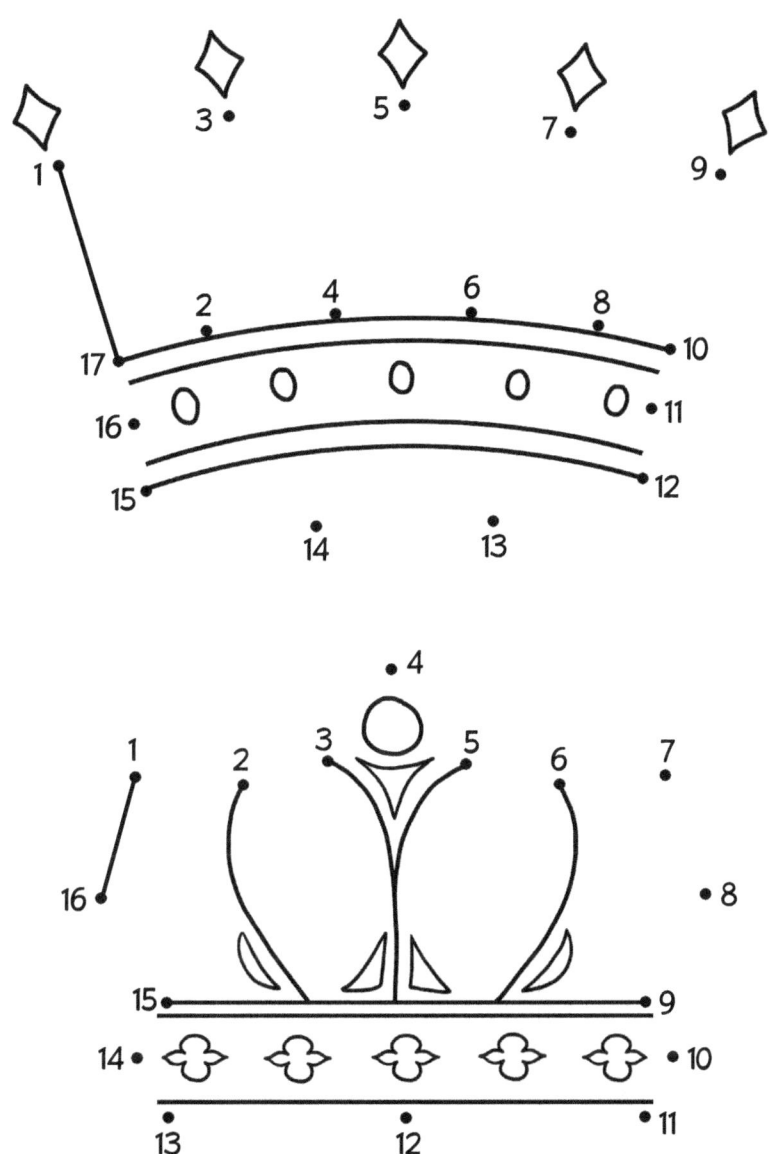

61

Three Brave Men

"Bow down to my golden statue!" commanded the king. But Shadrach, Meshach and Abednego only prayed and worshipped God. God kept them safe, even when the king threw them into the fire.

(Read Daniel 3)

A Secret Message

Use the fire codes below to fill in the blanks and find the secret message.

Daniel Prays to God

Daniel prayed to God three times a day. Daniel cared more about what God thought than what anyone else thought. God was pleased with Daniel and saved him from the hungry lions.

(Read Daniel 6)

Finish the Drawings

There are a few things missing from each lion. Find out what they are and draw them in.

65

Nehemiah Rebuilds

Nehemiah and God's people worked hard to rebuild the walls of the city. Some people tried to stop their work and bother them, but Nehemiah kept on working and did not give up.

(Read Nehemiah 1-4)

Finish the Job

Help Nehemiah find his bucket and tools to finish his job on the walls.

Brave Queen Esther

Queen Esther loved God very much. She prayed and asked God for courage to help her save her people. She wore fancy clothes and jewelry, but her real beauty was because of her loving heart.

(Read the Book of Esther)

Puzzle Pieces

Match the puzzle pieces by writing the matching numbers in the blank circles.

Jonah and the Fish

"Go to Nineveh," God told Jonah. "But I don't have time ... I don't want to ..." Jonah answered, as he went on a ship sailing the other way. Later, a mighty big fish taught Jonah a mighty important lesson.

(Read Jonah 1-3)

Raise the Sails!

Draw some of the things that Jonah may have seen on his trip.

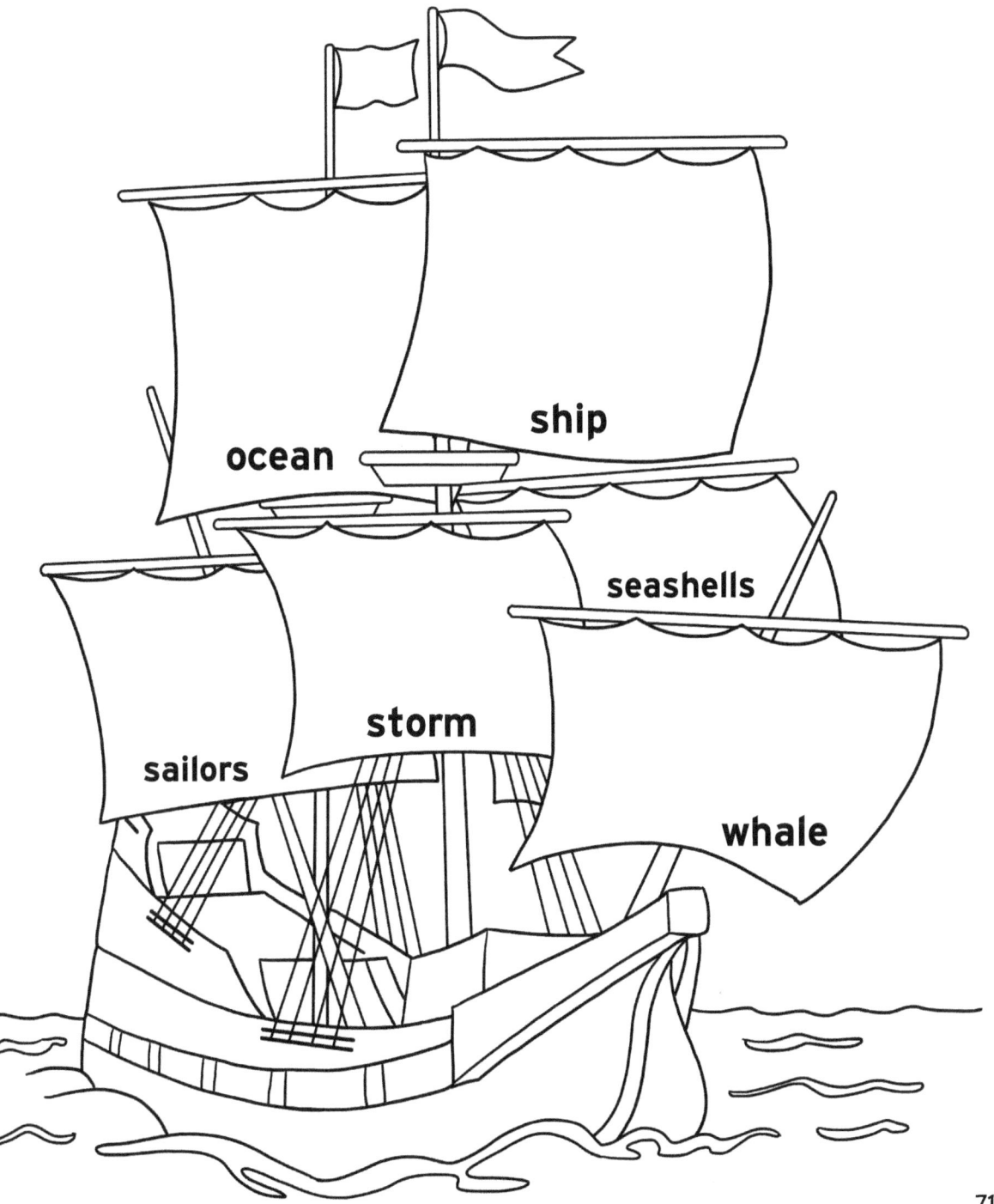

A King Is Born

Jesus was born in Bethlehem, in a simple place surrounded by animals.
We can thank God for sending His Son into the world that special night.

(Read Luke 2:6)

Make the Same

Draw the missing parts for the baby Jesus pictures. See the first picture as an example.

Sweet baby Jesus lay on a soft bed of hay.

The Wise Men Visit

The wise men followed the star that led them to Bethlehem where Jesus was born. They knelt down to worship and adore Him. They brought Him special gifts to show their thanks.

(Read Matthew 2:1-12)

Find the Gifts

Help the wise men pick the right gift for Jesus.

Jesus at the Temple

Jesus amazed the priests at the temple when He spoke about the Scriptures. Jesus was a good student and the more He listened to God, the more He grew in understanding.

(Read Luke 2:41-52)

Match the Shadows

Which shadow matches the picture of Jesus on the opposite page?

John Tells of Jesus

John the Baptist baptized people with the power of God. He didn't care what others thought about him. He spoke boldly and without fear, preparing the way for Jesus.

(Read John 1:19-34)

Puzzle Pieces

There are 3 different puzzles on this page. Draw a line to join the pieces that go together.

Jesus Picks 12 Disciples

Jesus was very busy teaching and helping people with their problems. So He chose twelve men to be His special helpers. They traveled with Him and did everything they could to be of service.

(Read Mark 3:13-19)

What's in the Net?

How many times can you find the word "fish" in the net?
Color in each word with a different color.

Hanging out with Jesus

Jesus had a lot of love to go around. He was kind to everyone, from the youngest baby to the oldest granddad. He took time to make each one feel loved in a special way.

(Read Matthew 19:13-15)

What's Different?

Find and circle ten differences between these two pictures.

Water to Wine

One day at a wedding party, the people ran out of something to drink. "What are we going to do?" they wondered. Jesus wanted to help them. He did a miracle and turned water into wine.

(Read John 2:1-11)

Amazing Miracle

Go through the maze as Jesus turns the water into wine.

Jesus Calms the Storm

"Help! Save us!" called the disciples during a great big storm. Jesus got up and told the storm to be quiet. Then He said, "Peace, peace!" Amazingly, the storm ended and all was quiet again.

(Read Mark 4:35-41)

Put in Order

Draw a line from the numbers to the circles to put the story in order.

- Jesus took a nap.
- The storm stopped.
- The disciples were afraid.
- Jesus calmed the storm.
- The disciples woke up Jesus.
- The waves hit the boat.
- Jesus and His disciples got on a boat.
- The wind blew harder and harder.

1
2
3
4
5
6
7
8

Doctor Jesus

A sad father ran to Jesus, "Please heal my little girl. I know You can do all things!" he pleaded. Jesus went to his home and because of the father's great faith, the little girl was better again.

(Read Mark 5:21-24, 35-43)

Finish the Picture

Draw yourself when you've been sick. How did you feel?
Then draw whoever took care of you and comforted you through it.
Now, imagine Jesus visiting and coming to heal you. Wouldn't that be great?

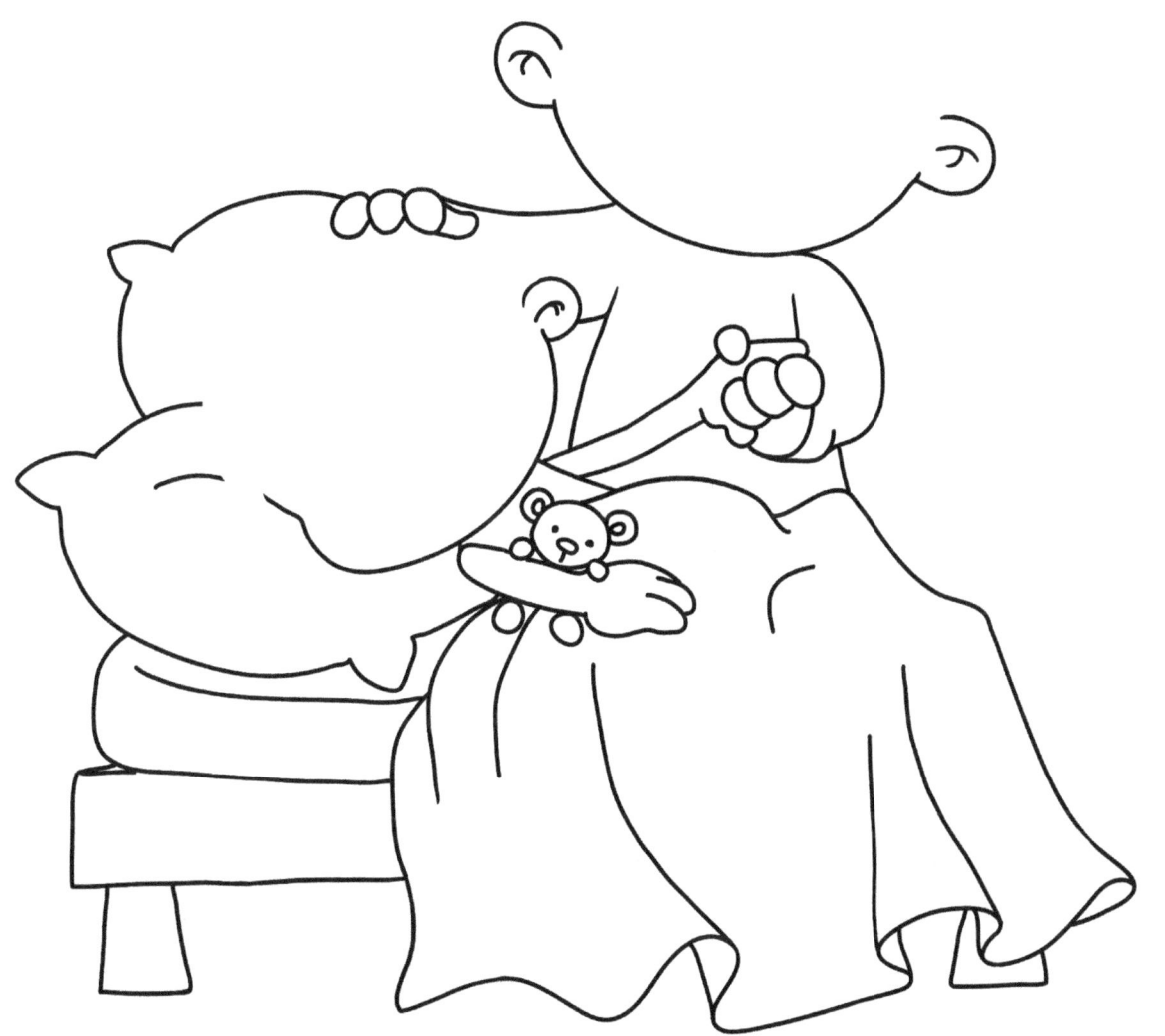

The Blind Can See

There was a man who couldn't see. "Help me please, Jesus. Help me!" he cried.
So Jesus healed him. The man saw the birds, the water and trees.

(Read Luke 18:35-43)

Make Them Glad

Color the faces. Then cut some "open eyes" and "happy smiles" from old magazines and glue them over the closed eyes and sad mouths.

A Lost Sheep Is Found

Jesus told a story of a shepherd who left his ninety-nine sheep to go and save just one that got lost. He found her stuck in thorns and he brought her home with love and care.

(Read Luke 15:1-7)

Hide-and-Seek

This lamb is playing hide-and-seek. Join the numbered dots to help find her.

The Lame Man

Some men carried their sick friend to Jesus. There was no place in the house and so they brought him down through the roof. Jesus healed the man and he could walk again.

(Read Mark 2:1-5)

Good Friends

Write the names of some of your friends in the boxes around the picture.
Then in the basket draw something that your friends did for you when you needed help.

A Boy Shares His Lunch

After listening to Jesus all day, the people got very hungry. One boy had a picnic meal with him and so he gave it to Jesus. Jesus blessed it and made it enough to feed thousands of people.

(Read John 6:1-14)

Moral of the Story

Find the matching fish and bread below and use the letters in each box to find the hidden message.

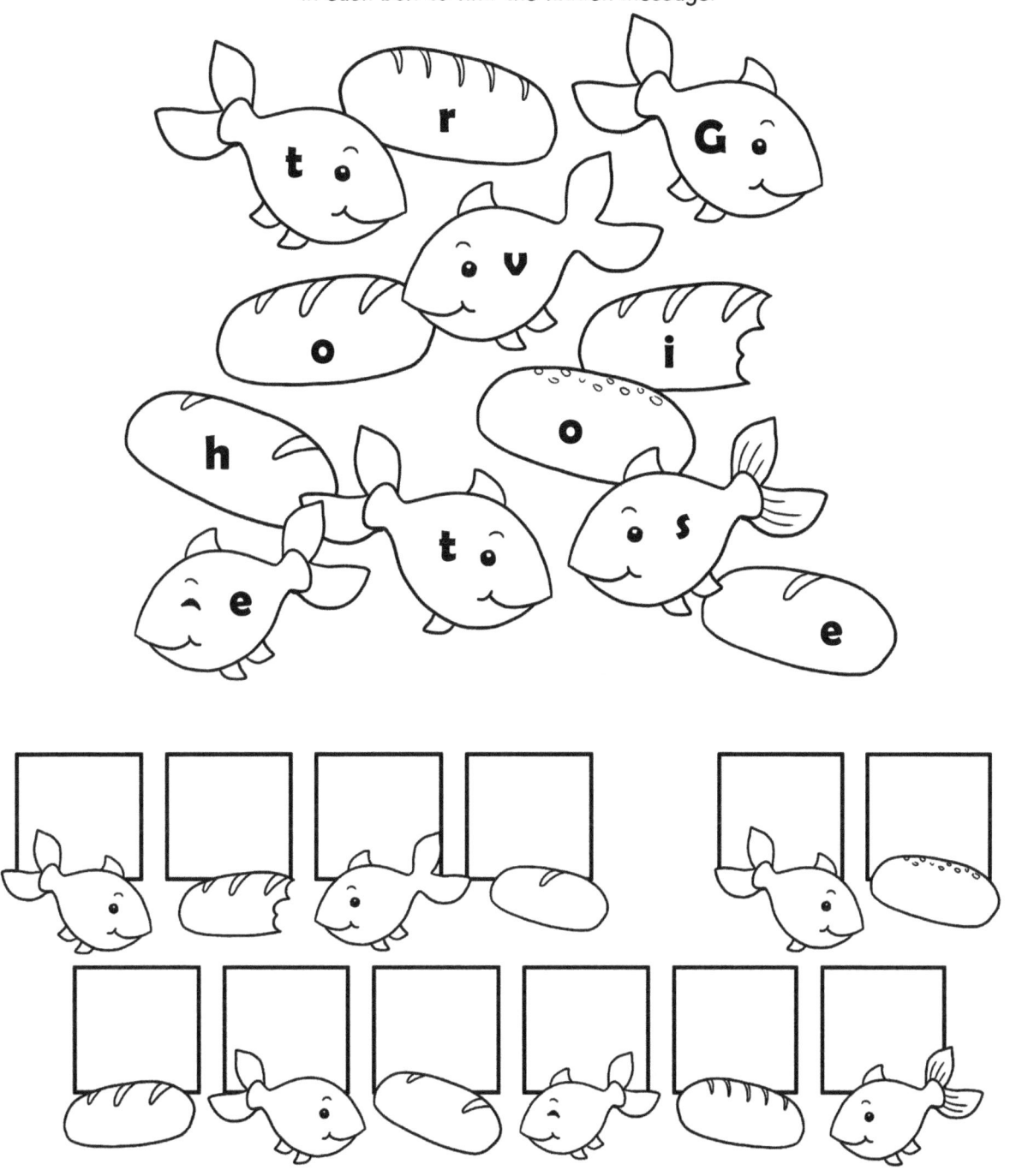

Stop to Listen

Mary stopped her work to listen to Jesus. But Martha got upset that Mary didn't help her with the cleaning and cooking. "Mary chose to put Me first," Jesus said. "That's the most important thing."

(Read Luke 10:38-42)

Guess Who?

Answer the questions by drawing a line to the correct pictures.

Who came for a visit?

Who is sitting still?

Who looks happy?

Who loves to spend time with us?

Who is working hard?

Who is preparing the meal?

Who looks upset?

Who should we put first?

Who took time to listen?

Jesus

Martha

Mary

A Samaritan

The traveler from Samaria stopped to help the wounded man who got robbed on the side of the road. He didn't just feel sorry for the man; he did his best to help him.

(Read Luke 10:30-37)

Follow the Path

Jesus told this story to teach us a lesson. Follow the path of letters to find out what it is.

The Party Boy

When a young man left home and wasted all his money he ended up with nothing. When he returned home, his dad showed him love and forgiveness.

(Read Luke 15:11-24)

Put in Order

Put these pictures in the right order by writing in the numbers 1-4.
Then color the pictures and tell the story in your own words.

The Thankful Man

Jesus healed ten lepers who were sick, but only one of them returned to show his thanks. Do you remember to thank Jesus for what He does for you?

(Read Luke 17:11-19)

Hidden Message

Color all the letters in the same color that have the same style of writing.
Then find the hidden message and write it in the box using your own style of writing.

Zacchaeus Is Sorry

Zacchaeus was a greedy, selfish man until he met Jesus. He was sorry for the bad that he had done and his life changed. Now he found a better way to live by giving to others.

(Read Luke 19:1-10)

Word Search

Find these words from the story in the Word Search.

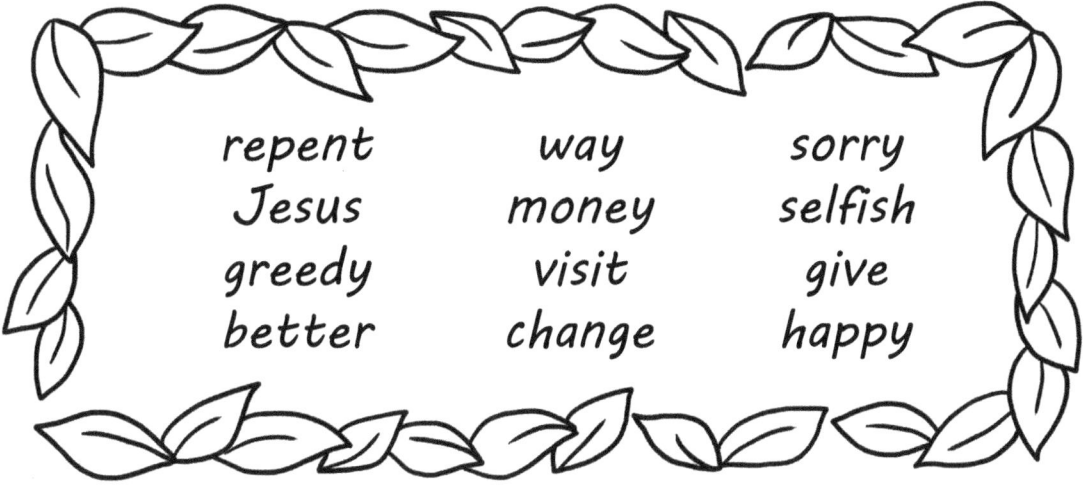

repent way sorry
Jesus money selfish
greedy visit give
better change happy

```
s a g r e e d y v a
t e w a y J h c i m
b r l l d e p h s o
g e h f r s e a i n
i p t a i u g n t e
v e u t p s w g u y
e n s m e p h e h r
t t s o r r y k z w
```

Into Jerusalem

As Jesus rode into Jerusalem, the people cheered and shouted for joy. They danced and sang and threw palm branches at His feet, as they did when greeting a king.

(Read Luke 19:28-40)

Clippety-Clop!

Sing "Hosanna!" as you follow the path to Jerusalem.

Not Just a Snack

Jesus and His helpers met for a special meal. He gave them each a piece of bread and a sip of wine. "When you eat and drink this, remember that I love you so much that I will give My life for you," Jesus said.

(Read 1 Corinthians 11:23-26; Matthew 26:26-30)

Find and Color

Find and color the pictures of the objects that Jesus asked us to remember Him by.

Jesus on the Cross

We have all made mistakes and done wrong, but Jesus had so much love that He died on the cross as a way to take our punishment for us. He made it possible for us to live with Him again in Heaven.

(Read Mark 15:1-39)

But Why?

Start the maze at the bottom with the question and find your way to the answer.

Jesus loves all His children. He died so that we could live with Him forever.

But why did Jesus have to die?

Write a little prayer here to thank Jesus for dying for you:

He Is Risen

Mary worried, "Oh no, where did they take my Jesus?" An angel said, "Don't worry. Jesus is alive again!" What wonderful news this was! She ran to share it with the others.

(Read John 20:1-18)

Wonderful News

Color and decorate this wonderful news.

Jesus Goes to Heaven

It was sad to see Jesus leave, but ... "I'm going to prepare a home in Heaven for you," Jesus said. "And one day, I will come again to take all My children home to live with Me forever."

(Read Luke 24:50-53; John 14:1-3)

Odd One Out

Match each cloud with its pair. There is one that doesn't have a pair. Which one is it? Draw a happy face on it.

Flames of Fire

The wind blew and a flame of fire that didn't burn landed on each one's head. "My heart is bubbling up with joy!" they said. This was God's Holy Spirit that Jesus had promised them.

(Read Acts 2:2-18)

Be the Artist

Draw a little flame of fire on each of the children's heads then finish drawing their bodies. Fill in the speech bubbles with how you think they might feel with God's Holy Spirit.

Good News to All

Jesus' helpers went everywhere telling others the good news of His love. From house to house, street to street and person to person; everyone needed to hear about Jesus.

(Read Matthew 28:18-20; Acts 2:43-47)

Many Ways

There are many different ways that you can be a witness to others.
Match the ideas and pictures.

I help pick up someone who got hurt.

I look for the good.

I give a smile.

I answer when someone calls for help.

I go and find someone to cheer up.

Heaven to Come

John (one of Jesus' disciples) wrote about the amazing things that he saw in Heaven. Now we can look forward to that wonderful day when we'll live with Jesus forever.

(Read Revelation 21-22)

John's Visions

Illustrate some of the things that John saw in his visions of Heaven.

Answer Sheet

Page 5
The hidden message is: <u>Male and Female</u>

Page 7

Page 9

Page 11
India/Hindi; Portugal/Portuguese; China/Chinese; Germany/German; England/English; Russia/Russian; France/French; Spain/Spanish; Greece/Greek

Page 13

Page 15
Abraham was <u>ninety-nine</u>

Page 17
Rebekah is sitting on the right-hand side

Page 19
Jacob learned about <u>trustworthiness</u>

Page 25

Page 29
1 = more; 2 = God; 3 = name;
4 = rest; 5 = respect; 6 = hurt;
7 = husband; 8 = things;
9 = truth; 10 = content

Page 31

Page 33

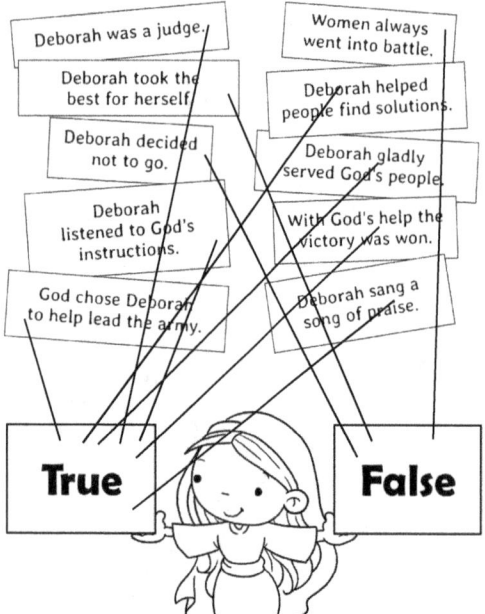

Page 35
The words that should be colored are:
Gideon, trust, ramshorn, tent, torch, night, jars, victory

Page 37
Samson got his true strength from <u>God</u>

Page 39
14

Page 41
Picture number 6

Page 43
Samuel <u>prayed</u>

Page 47

Page 49
The song comes from Psalm 23:1-2:
"The Lord is my shepherd; I shall not want.
He makes me to lie down in green pastures.
He leads me beside the still waters."

Page 51

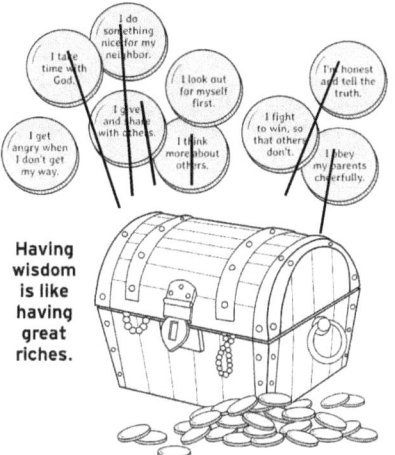

Having wisdom is like having great riches.

Page 57

Page 59

Page 63

The secret message is:
They only worshipped the true God

Page 67

Page 69

Page 75
1 = b; 2 = a; 3 = c

Page 77
Number 6 is Jesus' shadow.

Page 79

Page 81
The word "fish" appears 6 times.

Page 83

Page 85

Page 87
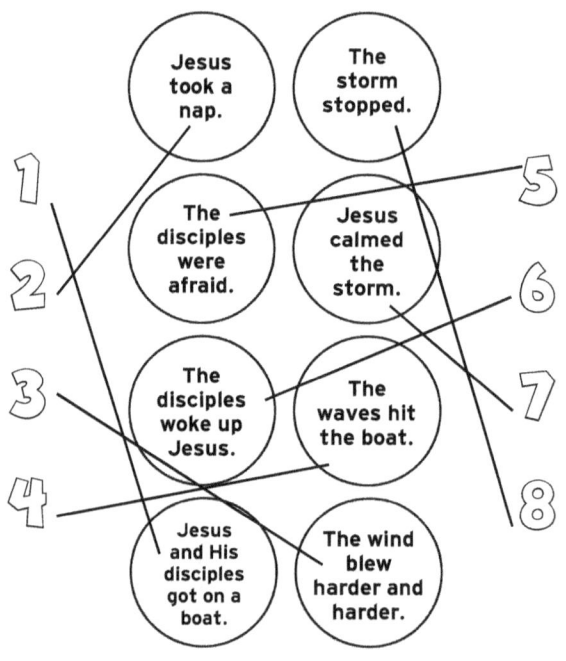

127

Page 97
The hidden message is "Give to others".

Page 99

- Who came for a visit? — Jesus
- Who is sitting still? — Mary
- Who looks happy? — Mary
- Who loves to spend time with us? — Jesus
- Who is working hard? — Martha
- Who is preparing the meal? — Martha
- Who looks upset? — Martha
- Who should we put first? — Jesus
- Who took time to listen? — Mary

Page 101
The lesson that Jesus teaches us is "be a good neighbor".

Page 103
3, 2, 4, 1

Page 105
The hidden message is "Thank you".

Page 107

Page 109

Page 111

Page 113

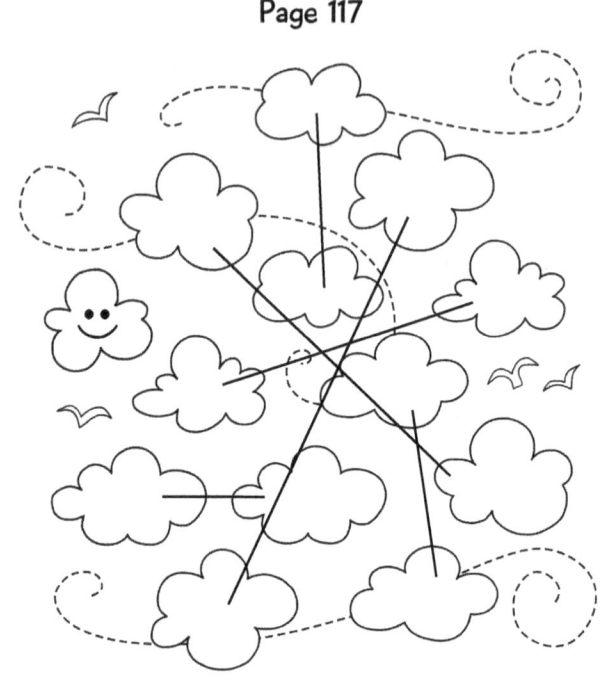

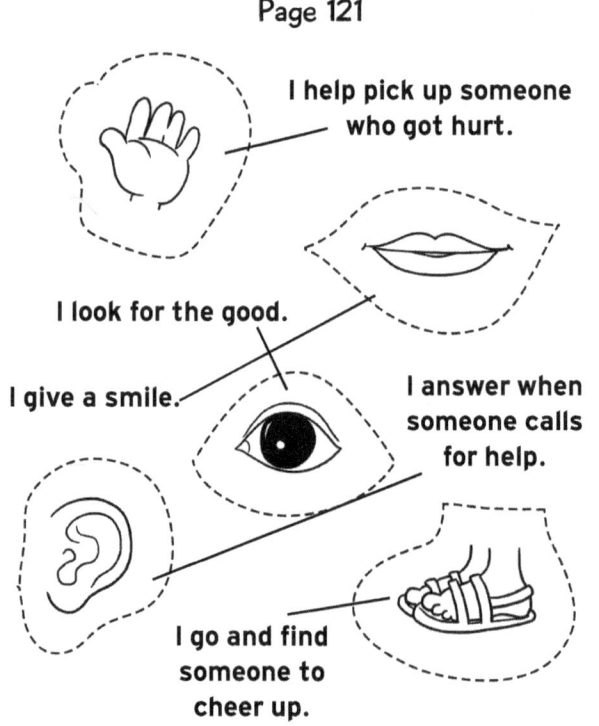

www.ingramcontent.com/pod-product-compliance
Lightning Source LLC
Chambersburg PA
CBHW081428070526
44586CB00020B/2522